How To
KNIT

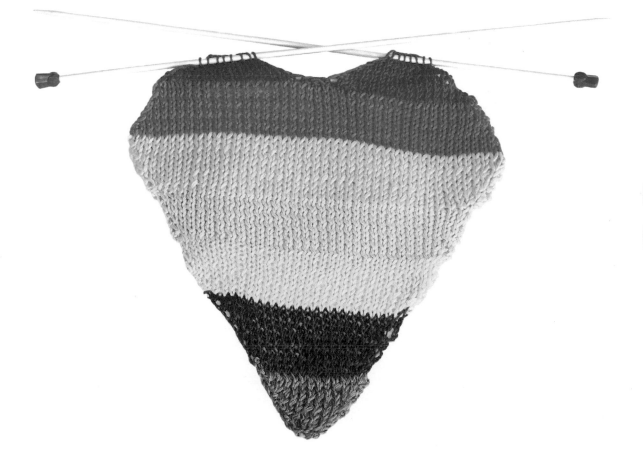

A Complete Guide
for Absolute Beginners

Alison McNicol

First published in 2013 by Kyle Craig Publishing
Text and illustration copyright © 2013 Kyle Craig Publishing

Design and illustration: Julie Anson

ISBN : ISBN: 978-1-908707-26-0
A CIP record for this book is available from the British Library.

A Kyle Craig Publication
www.kyle-craig.com

Contents

All About Knitting

Stitches

Projects

All About Knitting!

Welcome to How To Knit: A Complete Guide for Absolute Beginners.

Knitting has risen hugely in popularity in recent years and, as with crochet and sewing, is no longer seen as an "old granny" pastime. A whole new generation of young women — and perhaps even men! — are discovering how fun and easy it is to pick up a pair of knitting needles and some yarn and create something beautiful.

This book is aimed at the absolute beginner, so don't worry if you have never tried to knit before — the clear and easy to follow illustrations and pictures here will help you get started and have you knitting your first stitches in no time!

I've chosen a lovely selection of projects that are easy enough for complete novices to make in a relatively short space of time, and that progress your skills as you move on through the book, so whether you're hoping to make cute knitted gifts for friends, beautiful knitted accessories for your home, or have your heart set on a big chunky knitted blanket, there's sure to be a project here to inspire you.

So — what are you waiting for? Read on, follow the steps provided, and you'll be delighted to discover just how easy it is to learn to knit!

Happy knitting!

Alison x

Tools

As well as knitting needles and yarn, there are a few other things you will need to help you complete your projects. Why not make yourself a nice basket or box where you can keep all your knitting and sewing tools together?

Sewing Basket
When it is time to sew your projects together, you will need scissors, large tapestry or darning needles, and some thread. You will also need a tape measure to help you measure your work, and it's always nice to have lovely buttons and things too.

Row Counter
With some projects you may have to knit a certain number of rows. A row counter fits on the end of your needle and you can turn the dial to adjust the number at the end of each row to remind you how many rows you have knitted so far.

Needle Point Protectors
These fit over the point of your needles to stop your stitches sliding off when you put your knitting down.

Stitch Holder
A stitch holder is a bit like a giant safety pin and can be used to hold your stitches together while you shape your knitting, or when you need to use the needles for another project.

Needle Size Guide

Metric(mm)	US	UK/Canadian
2.0	0	14
2.25	1	13
2.5	-	-
2.75	2	12
3	-	11
3.25	3	10
3.5	4	-
3.75	5	9
4.0	6	8
4.5	7	7
5.0	8	6
5.5	9	5
6	10	4
6.5	10.5	3
7	-	2
7.5	-	1
8.0	11	0
9.0	13	00
10.0	15	000

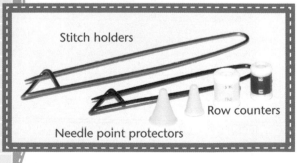

Stitch holders

Row counters

Needle point protectors

Yarns

When you first go shopping for yarn/wool you will notice that as well as a fantastic range of colours to choose from there is a dazzling array of types, thicknesses and weights available.

It's important to choose the correct weight of yarn for the project that you're making, and most patterns should tell you the size of needles to use **AND** the type or weight of yarn required.

Usually the weight or type of yarn is printed on the label — also known as the ball band — that is wrapped around it. The label will tell you the weight of the yarn, the tension, the washing instructions, and the most suitable needle size to use.

If you are knitting a project that will use more than one ball of yarn, you should also check for the **'dye lot'** number on the band to ensure they are all the exact same colour.

Wool/Yarn Guide

	Lace	Super Fine	Fine	Light	Medium	Chunky
Yarn weight	0	1	2	3	4	5
Common use	Lace	Baby clothes, decorative items	Socks, baby clothes	Light scarves, accessories	Mittens, scarves, toys etc,	Blankets, scarves, winter items
Tension range Stocking Stitch (stitches per 10cm/4")	33–40 St st	27–32 St st	23–26 St st	21–24 St st	16–20 St st	12–15 St st
Recommended Needle Size (UK/US):	1.5-2.25mm/ 000-1	2.25-3.25mm/ 1-3	3.25-3.75mm/ 3-5	3.75-4.5mm/ 5-7	4.5-5.5mm/ 7-9	5.5-8 mm/ 9-11

Knitting Terminology

Once you move on from this book, regular knitting patterns or instructions will feature a host of abbreviations and knitting terminology. We will use them, together with fuller explanations, throughout this book to get you used to them and prepare you for regular patterns.

Some knitting terms are different in the UK to the US — this book uses the UK terminology throughout — for US readers, please see the US terms below.

UK term	US term
4ply yarn	sport yarn
Aran yarn	12-ply/worsted/fisherman yarn – a thick, chunky yarn
Cast off	bind off
Cast on	bind on
Chunky yarn	Bulky yarn
DK (double-knit) yarn	5-6ply/light worsted – a medium-weight yarn
Stocking stitch	stockinette stitch
Moss stitch(british)	seed stitch
Tension	gauge
Wool	yarn

alt	alternate	p	purl
beg	beginning	p1	purl 1 stitch
cm	centimetres	p1, k1	purl 1 stitch, then knit 1 stitch
cont	continue / continuing	p2tog	purl the next 2 stitches together
dec	decrease	p3tog	purl the next 3 stitches together
dk	double knitting, a medium-weight yarn / light worsted (US term)	patt	pattern
		rep	repeat
foll	following/follows	rh	right hand
g	gramme(s)	rs	right side
in	inches	ss	slip stitch
inc	increase	st(s)	stitch(es)
k	knit	st st	stocking/stockinette stitch
k1	knit 1 stitch	tog	together
k1, p1	knit 1 stitch, then purl 1 stitch	ws	wrong side
k2tog	knit the next 2 stitches together	yf	yarn forward: bring the yarn to the front of work, between the needles, then over the top of the right needle to make a new stitch
k3tog	knit the next 3 stitches together		
mm	millimetre(s)	yo	yarn over – US term for yarn forward, above
oz	ounce(s)		

Making Pom Poms

Pom poms are so fun and easy to make and can be used on all sorts of projects — on hats, scarves, bags and more!

All you need is some cardboard and yarn, and some round lids or shapes to draw around, and you're all set to make pom poms!

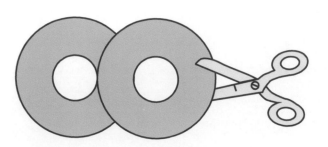

Step 1: How large would you like your pom pom? Find a jar lid, CD or something of similar size and draw around it on the cardboard. Now draw a smaller circle inside the large one. Repeat this, so that you cut two cardboard "donuts" that are both the same.

Step 2: If you are using a large ball of yarn, it will be too big to pass through the hole, so make a small ball that will fit by winding the yarn around your fingers lots of times. Stop before it is too large to fit through the hole.

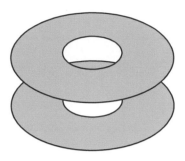

Step 3: Now put both discs together. You're now ready to start winding your yarn around the discs.

Step 4: Holding the two discs together, start winding your yarn over the disc and through the hole, repeating again and again until you have covered the whole disc in yarn. Keep repeating this until the hole is too small for any more yarn to pass through.

Step 5: Carefully insert one blade of your scissors between the two discs, and start cutting through the yarn. Keep moving the scissors around the edge, cutting the yarn as you go, until you have cut all the way around.

Step 6: Cut a length of yarn and carefully pull apart the two discs slightly. Wrap your yarn between the two discs and around the middle of your pom pom, and tie in a tight knot. Do this a couple more times so that your pom pom is really secure. Now rip or cut each disc away, and roll your pom pom between your hands to hide the join and make it nice and fluffy!

Making a Slip Knot

Before we can "Cast on" some stitches to knit, we need to start with a Slip Knot.

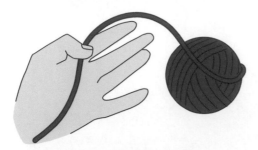

Step 1: Unravel some yarn from the ball, and grip the loose end between your thumb and your hand, with your palm facing towards you.

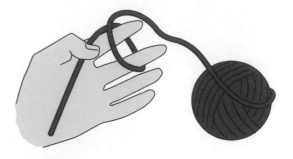

Step 2: Now wrap the yarn (from the ball end, not the loose end) in a loop around your first two fingers.

Step 3: Using your right hand, reach through this loop and pull some more yarn from the ball through — this will form a new loop.

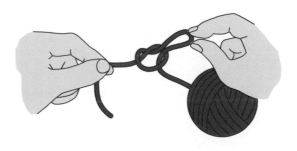

Step 4: Hold onto this loop with your right hand, and pull gently on the loose end with your left hand. Now you're ready to slide your slip knot onto your needle!

Casting On

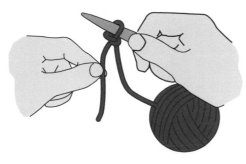

Step 1: Slide the slip knot onto one of your needles and gently pull on the loose end to tighten it. From this point on you will always be using the ball end of the yarn, not the loose end.

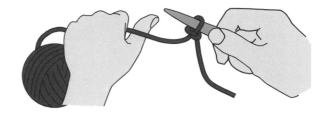

Step 2: Holding your needle in one hand, grip the working end (the end that leads to the ball) of the yarn with the other hand.

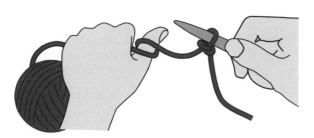

Step 3: Wrap the yarn in a loop around your thumb.

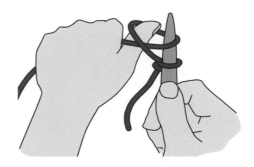

Step 4: Push your needle tip through this loop, slide your thumb out, and pull the working end of the yarn to tighten.

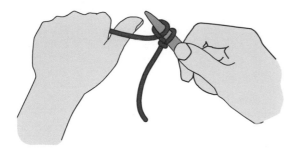

Step 5: You have now Cast on a new stitch. Repeat Steps 2-4 until you have the correct amount of stitches that your project suggests. Why not cast on 20, ready for some practice knitting?

Step 6: And now you have 20 stitches, ready to start KNITTING!

Knit Stitch

Knit stitch is the most basic and simple of all knitting stitches, so it's the obvious first stitch to learn!

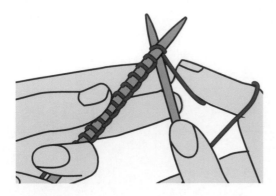

Step 1: Hold the needle that has the cast-on stitches in your left hand, and the empty needle in your right hand. Push the point of your right hand needle up into the first stitch, from front to back.

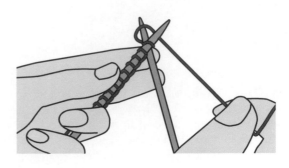

Step 2: Now wrap the *working end* of the yarn around the back of the right hand needle, then around the right hand needle and between the tips of the two needles.

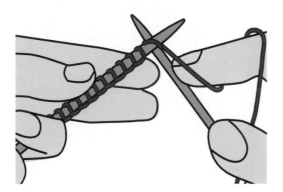

Step 3: Holding the yarn tight, slide your right hand needle towards you, down through the stitch on the left needle.

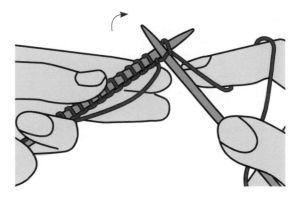

Step 4: Slide your right hand needle up so that the stitch on the left needle slips off, and the new stitch stays on your right needle.

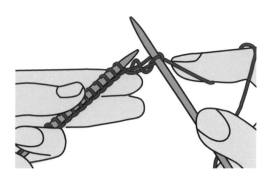

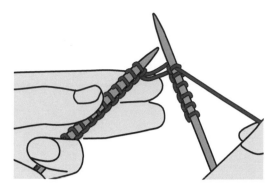

Step 5: You will now have a loop on your right hand needle. Well done, you've just knitted a new stitch!

Step 6: Pull your yarn to tighten the stitch, then repeat steps 2–6 until all the stitches from the left needle have been knitted over to your right needle.

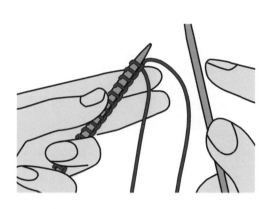

Step 7: Now you have knitted your first ROW! Swap your needles so that the one with all the stitches is back in your left hand.

Step 8: Keep knitting row after row and watch as your knitting grows and grows!

When we use Knit stitch for **every** stitch and **every** row, both sides will look exactly the same. This is also known as **Garter stitch!**

The 'working end' of the yarn is the yarn that is coming directly from the ball of yarn!

Purl Stitch

Purl stitch is used in combination with Knit stitch to produce various other knitting stitches and styles. On the next page, we will be using Knit stitch and Purl stitch to create Stocking stitch — so let's learn how to Purl!

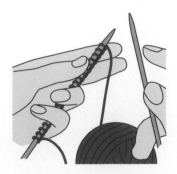

Step 1: Cast on 20 stitches using the same method as on page 11. As usual, hold the needle with the cast on stitches in your left hand, the empty needle in your right.

Step 2: With your yarn in front of the needles, not behind, insert your right hand needle into the front of the first stitch, so that your right needle crosses over the left needle.

Step 3: Wrap the working end of the yarn over the tip of the right needle, from right to left, so that it looks like this.

Step 4: Slide the tip of your right needle down and away from you, pushing it through the centre of the stitch on the left needle. You will now see a loop on your right needle.

Step 5: Keep sliding your right needle so that the original stitch slides off the left needle, but you keep the new stitch on your right needle. Well done, you've now made your first Purl stitch!

Step 6: To Purl the whole row, repeat stages 2–5 until you have knitted all the stitches on the left needle over to the right needle.

Step 7: If you needed to purl the next row, simply swap needles so that the needle with the stitches is in your left hand, then repeat stages 2–5 until you have purled another row… and so on.

Stocking Stitch

When we knit alternate rows of Knit stitch and Purl stitch, we create Stocking stitch. This is also sometimes called Stockinette stitch. This is a pretty stitch and looks smoother on the front side and bumpier on the back. The smooth side will look like a row of tiny "V's", and the back will look like regular knit stitch. Let's practice Stocking stitch.

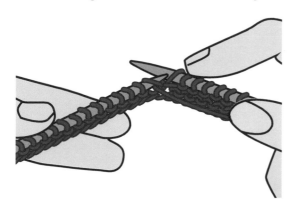

Step 1: Cast on 20 stitches as before, and knit the whole row using Knit stitch.

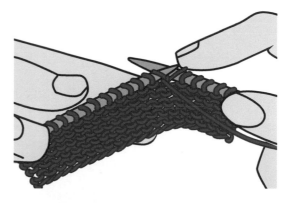

Step 2: Bring the yarn to the front and do the next row in Purl stitch.

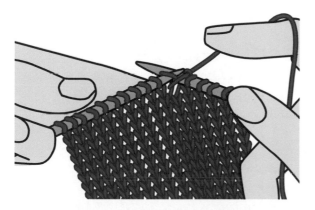

Step 3: Keep doing alternate rows of Knit stitch, then Purl stitch. You will notice that one side of your knitting is smooth V's", and the other side is bumpy.

Tip!

If you lose track of whether you knit the last row or purled it, look at your knitting. Hold your needles in the ready-to-knit position (with the left hand needle holding the stitches) and look at what's facing you. If you're looking at the smooth side, you use Knit stitch for the next row. If you're looking at the bumpy side, you purl the next row. **Easy!**

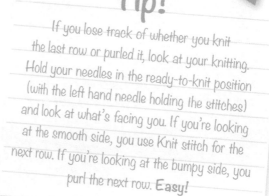

Rib Stitch

Rib stitch — sometimes called Ribbing — is another cool combination of Knit stitch and Purl stitch.

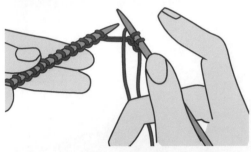

Step 1: Cast on 20 stitches. Knit the first two in Knit stitch. Then bring your yarn forward between the two needles ready for Purl stitch.

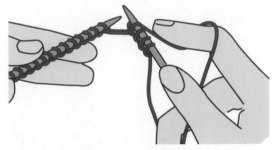

Step 2: With your yarn now in front, Purl the next two stitches. Then take the yarn back behind your needles ready for Knit stitch.

Step 3: Continue alternating two Knit stitches, then two Purl stitches until you have reached the end of your stitches. You should have ended on two Purl stitches.

Step 5: Once you have done a few rows, you will start to see the ribbed pattern!

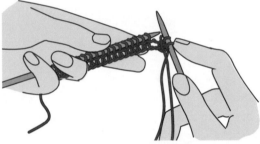

Step 4: Move the needle with the stitches on to your left hand, and begin again. Start with two Knit stitches, then two Purl stitches and so on. Don't forget to have your yarn at the **BACK** for Knit stitch, and at the **FRONT** for Purl stitch!

Lost track of what stitch you should do next? If the next two stitches are bumpy, you need to *purl*. If not, *knit*!

Rib stitch consists of columns of Knit stitches alternating with columns of Purl stitches. To make a ribbed pattern, you change from Knit stitches to Purl stitches within a row. You should always cast on an EVEN number of stitches i.e. 20, 22, 28, 40 etc. when knitting Rib stitch.

To create 2x2 ribbing, cast on a multiple of 4 stitches i.e. 16, 20, 24, 28 etc. Then knit 2 stitches, purl 2 stitches, knit 2, purl 2 on each row. You can also try creating narrower or broader columns of ribbing using other combinations (always of EVEN numbers of stitches i.e. 1x1, 2x2, 4x4 etc.).

Moss Stitch

Moss stitch is another great combination of Knit stitch and Purl stitch. Moss stitch is a pattern created by alternately working one Knit stitch and one Purl stitch on every row. The Purl stitch is then worked over the Knitted stitch on the next row.

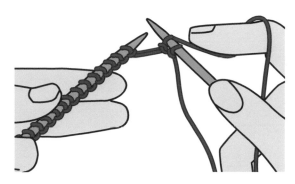

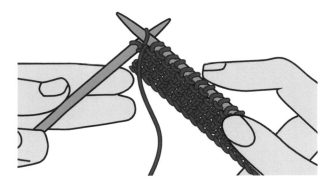

Step 1: Cast on an *EVEN* number of stitches. Knit one stitch, then bring your yarn forward ready to purl.

Step 2: Carry on alternating a Knit stitch then a Purl stitch until you reach the end of the row. Because you cast on an *EVEN* number of stitches, your last stitch will be a Purl stitch. Don't forget to have your yarn at the *BACK* for Knit stitch, and at the *FRONT* for Purl stitch!

This version is also known as Seed stitch or British Moss stitch. Row 1: K,P,K,P to end.
Row 2: P,K,P,K to end.
Continue to alternate each row as above.

Step 3: For your next row, start on a Purl (P) stitch, then a Knit (K) stitch, then continue to alternate each stitch with P,K,P,K to the end.

Step 4: Continue to alternate each row so that one row begins on a Knit (K) stitch, the next begins on a Purl (P) stitch and you alternate the Knit and Purl stitches within the row.

Lost track of what stitch you should do next? If the stitch on the row below is bumpy, do a *knit* stitch. If not, *purl*!

17

Changing Colours

Using a single colour of yarn is fine for your first projects, but after a while you could try something a little more interesting. A fun and easy technique for adding interest to your knitted items is adding stripes.

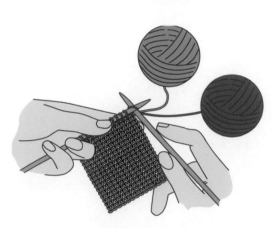

Step 1: When you have finished an even number of rows (2, 4, 6 etc. — your pattern should tell you how many), leave the ball attached and just start knitting with the next colour. To add the new colour, leave a few inches of tail, hold it tight as you would hold the yarn to begin a regular row, and begin knitting.

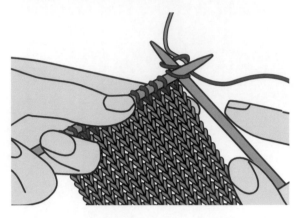

Step 2: The next time you get to that side (which would be after 2 rows, but it could even be after 4, 6, 8 or more even rows, depending on your pattern) pick up the old colour, wrap the yarn you're working with around it and go on knitting with the old colour. This will secure the yarn to the side of the project and move it up to where you'll need it next.

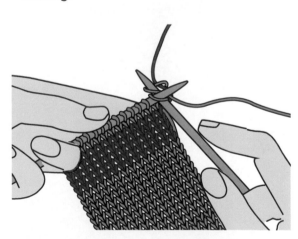

Step 3: Repeat this process for each new stripe, so that the yarn is carried up the side each time.

Step 4: Hurrah, you've made some stripes!

Joining Yarn

At some point during a project you may find that you will soon run out of yarn — you've used the whole ball — so you need to start using a fresh ball of the same yarn. To do this you need to "join" your yarn. Here's how:

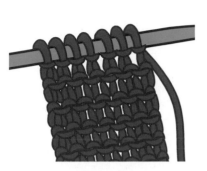

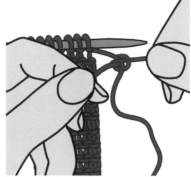

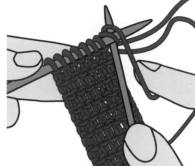

Step 1: You should always aim to join your yarn at the end of a row, not in the middle. So finish the row you are working on, and leave at least 6 inches/15cm of yarn from the first ball. You will need this much to tie it onto the new ball.

Step 2: Using a loose knot, tie the old yarn to the end of the new ball, making your knot as close to the edge of your knitting as possible.

Step 3: Now you can start using the new ball of yarn to knit with. Don't worry about the loose end from the old yarn, here's how you can sew in this loose end once you have finished the knitting.

Sewing in Loose Ends

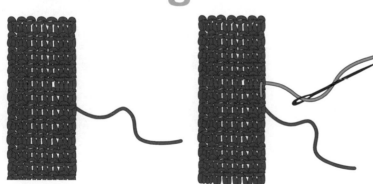

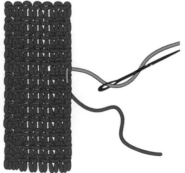

Step 1: Use a needle with a large enough eye for your loose yarn to be threaded through. Thread the needle with the loose yarn, and sew one stitch to the row above, close to the edge of the knitting.

Step 2: Pull the yarn through, then make a new stitch into the row above, close to the edge again.

Step 3: Keep stitching like this until you have either done 6 stitches, or your yarn has run out. After 6 stitches, cut the end from the yarn as it is now secure enough. Be VERY careful not to cut into your knitting accidentally!

Increasing

Increasing the number of stitches is a way to either make your knitting wider, or to create shapes in your knitting. There are a couple of ways to do this, and which way to increase will depend on the shape you are making and what the pattern tells you to do.

Increasing at the beginning of a row

This is sometimes also called a **Cable Increase** and can be used to add one or more extra stitches at the beginning of a row.

Step 1: Slip the tip of your right needle in between the first two stitches of the left needle.

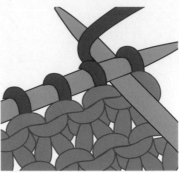

Step 2: Wrap the working end of the yarn under and around the right needle. Hold the yarn tight.

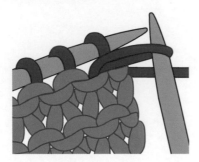

Step 3: Now draw the right needle towards you, pulling it through and under the two stitches on the left needle. You will now have a new loop on your right needle.

Step 4: Now slide this new loop onto your left needle, at the end. You have now increased by one stitch.

Step 5: If your pattern tells you to add more than one stitch at this point, do so, then continue knitting as normal.

Increasing anywhere in a row

This is also called a **Bar increase** and is good for adding a single extra stitch anywhere within a row. You can only add one extra stitch at a time using this method.

 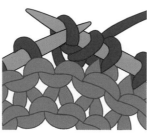  

Step 1: Knit a stitch as usual, but do not slide the stitch off the left hand needle like you would usually.

Step 2: Now slip your right needle into the *BACK* of this same stitch on your left needle.

Step 3: Knit this stitch again. You will now have two more stitches on your right needle.

Step 4: Now you can slip the original stitch off the left needle like you would usually. You have now increased your knitting by one extra stitch.

Decreasing

By decreasing the number of stitches, you can make your knitting narrower. Decreasing removes stitches, narrowing the knitting.

Decrease Method 1: Knitting 2 Together

This method of decreasing can be used anywhere in a row — at the beginning, middle or end. You can decrease by just one stitch each time this way. Slip your right needle into two stitches on your left needle, instead of one. Knit them both together as though they were just one stitch. You have now decreased by one stitch and can continue knitting according to your pattern.

Decrease Method 2: Casting-off

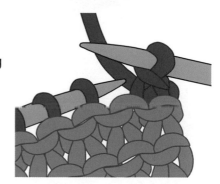

This method can be used to decrease stitches at the beginning or end of a row, not in the middle. It uses the same technique as Casting off at the very end of your knitting — turn over to page 20 for more details. You would follow Step 1 and Step 2 for each stitch you needed to decrease by.

Casting Off

Once you have finished a piece of knitting you need to secure the stitches and ends of your yarn so that it does not unravel. This is done by using a method called **Casting Off**.

Step 1: Knit two stitches, then slide the tip of your left needle into the front of the first stitch you knitted onto your right needle.

Step 2: Now carefully lift that first stitch over the second stitch, and slip it off the tip of the right needle. Pull your yarn tight.

Step 3: Slide out your left needle, and now you will have just one stitch left on the right needle. Now knit over one more stitch from the left needle onto the right, so that you have 2 stitches on the right needle again.

Step 5: Keep doing this until you are left with just one stitch on your left needle.

Step 4: Repeat Step 2, slipping the first stitch over the second stitch and off the right needle. Keep knitting a second stitch onto the right needle, and reducing it to one using Step 2. You should only ever have 2 stitches at a time on the right needle, ready to reduce to one stitch.

Step 6: Cut the yarn, leaving about 6 inches/15cm and pull the end of the yarn through the final stitch (it may help to pull the left needle away so that the stitch becomes a larger loop). Pull tightly, and your knitting has now been safely cast off and secured!

Oops! Dropped Stitches

When you first start knitting, it's easy to accidentally drop the odd stitch. If this happens, don't worry, it's pretty easy to fix!

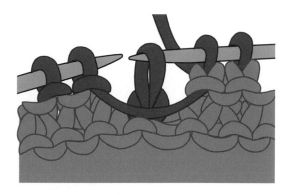

Step 1: Can you see where the dropped stitch has slipped to? Catch it with the tip of your right needle, slipping the needle tip through the stitch.

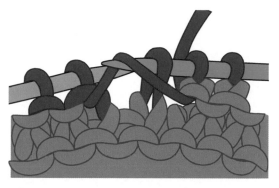

Step 2: Now can you see a loose strand of yarn which should have been part of your new stitch. Slip the tip of your right needle under this too.

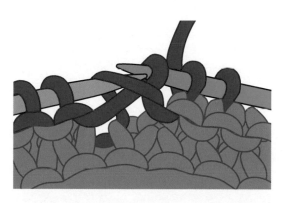

Step 3: Now you will need your left needle to help with the job! Use the tip of the left needle to slip under the dropped stitch (which is now on your right needle) and pull it over the strand that you also caught, then let it drop off the right needle. A lot like when you Bind-off or Cast off. You now have the proper stitch on your right needle.

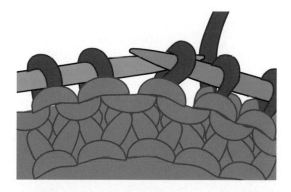

Step 3: But this stitch actually needs to be on your left needle so that you can "knit" it properly. So use your left needle to help slide it over onto the left needle. Now you have "caught" the dropped stitch and it is ready to be knitted as normal. Hurrah!

Sewing Together

Once you have knitted all the parts of a project, it will be time to sew them together. Usually you will want your stitches to be hidden, so you should use a large darning or tapestry needle and the same yarn to sew the pieces together. You may already know some sewing stitches, but here's a new one used especially in knitting and crochet – **mattress stitch**. This stitch is a great way to sew together knitted pieces as invisibly as possible. When sewing knitting together, always use a large tapestry needle (make sure your tapestry needle is blunt to avoid piercing the yarn).

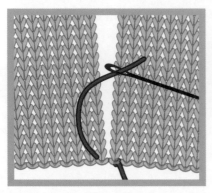

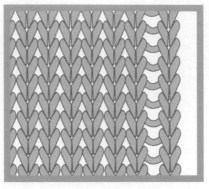

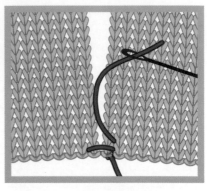

Step 1: Lay the pieces you wish to join on a flat surface, side by side, with the *wrong side,* (the inside) facing up. Thread your needle with the same yarn, then secure it to the end of your knitted work with a couple of stitches on top of each other.

Step 2: Now look closely at the knitting and gently pull apart the first two edge stitches. Can you see the series of little horizontal running threads connecting them? We will be using these for our mattress stitches.

Step 3: Put your needle under and through the horizontal running thread that runs between the first and second stitch on the opposite piece of knitting, like in this diagram. Pull your yarn all the way through.

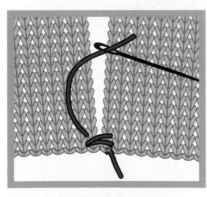

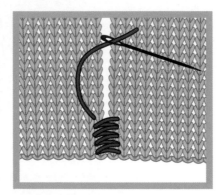

Step 4: Cross over to the other piece of knitting and do the same, on the same stitch, on that side. Pull the yarn through again. Carry on like this, zig zagging from one piece to the other, moving up one stitch each time.

Step 5: Each time you make a stitch and pull on the yarn tight, you will be creating a strong "seam" to hold your work together. When you reach the end, secure with 2 or 3 stitches on top of each other.

The **RIGHT SIDE** is the side of your knitted piece that you want on display. The **WRONG SIDE** will be the back, or the inside, of your knitted item.

Sewing On Buttons

Once you have knitted something, you may want to add buttons to look like eyes, or just to make it prettier.

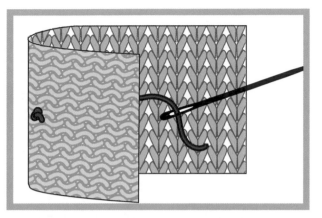

Step 1: Thread your needle with matching yarn or thread and tie a knot at the far end. (Before doing this, double check that the eye of your needle fits through the holes in your button. If not, use a smaller needle!) Decide where you want your button to be, and bring your needle up through the middle of that area, from the rear of the crochet so that the needle comes out on the **RIGHT** side.

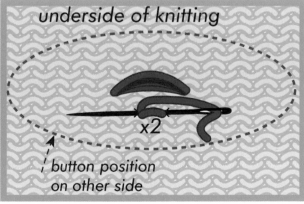

Step 2: Now sew two small stitches on top of each other. This will secure your thread or yarn to the knitting before you start sewing on your button.

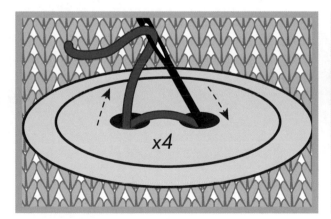

Step 3: Grab your button and place it over the area it will go. Now bring your needle and thread up through one hole of the button. Pull thread all the way. Next go down through the other hole, again pulling thread all the way. Do this 4 times, or until it no longer feels wobbly when you tug on it.

Step 4: On the underside of the knitting, just underneath where the button now is, do two or three small stitches to secure your thread or yarn. You have now sewn on your button and can cut the extra yarn off. Be **VERY** careful not to cut into your knitting!

Projects

Funky Chunky Scarf

STITCH
St st
Stocking Stitch
USED

For your very first project, we're going to knit something that doesn't require you to follow a complicated, rigid pattern. This will allow you to practice knitting and get used to holding your needles, tensioning your yarn and perfecting your first knitting stitches .

This scarf uses **Stocking Stitch** — where you knit a row, then purl a row, knit a row, purl a row and so on — so it's a great way to practice your first two stitch styles.

For a scarf like this a chunky, bulky aran-weight yarn is a great choice PLUS it knits up much quicker than finer yarns.

You will need:

1 pair of 8mm needles (US size 11)

2 x 100g balls of chunky aran-weight yarn

How to knit:

Cast On 20 stitches.

Row 1: k20 (knit all 20 stitches)

Row 2: p20 (purl all 20 stitches)

Then simply continue alternating a row of knit stitch with a row of purl stitch until the scarf is as long as desired.

Cast off.

TIP!
Try sewing the 2 short ends together to make a cool "circular" style scarf wrap?

TIP!
For a child-sized scarf, cast on just 10 or 15 stitches.

TIP!
Make a large pom pom for each end for a fun, retro look.

# Fingerless Mittens

STITCH
St st
Stocking Stitch
USED

These gorgeous mittens are so easy to knit and can be adapted in all sorts of ways. They can be knitted in pretty much any stitch you like — how about Stocking stitch or Moss stitch? — and you could even create cool stripy ones with leftover yarn.

For your first pair use a simple Stocking stitch and one colour of yarn so they are incredibly easy to make.

You will need:

1 pair of 4.5 mm knitting needles

Aran weight yarn
(approx. 60g per pair of mittens)

Buttons, bows, fabric/wool flowers to decorate

How to knit:

Cast on 40 stitches.

Start with a row of Knit stitch, followed by a row of Purl stitch, alternating with each row. Continue until your work measures 15cm/6 in.

Cast off, leaving a short tail around 10cm/4 in long.

You will now have one knitted rectangle, which will make a mitten. Do the same again to create a second rectangle.

Making up Fingerless Mittens:

Step 1: Lay your knitted rectangle with the right side (the nice side) facing up, and the Cast On and Cast off edges running across the top and bottom of rectangle. Grab the left edge and fold in half, lengthways. Now place your hand on top.

Step 2: Notice where your thumb sticks out — this will be where you need to leave a hole in your joining up. You can mark where to stop sewing by putting safety pins at the top and bottom of the hole. You can now use the 10cm/4 in tail you left to sew the top section.

Step 3: Sew the sides up using mattress stitch (see **page 24**), remembering that gap for your thumb! Don't forget to secure the stitches with 2 or 3 stitches on top of each other at the beginning and the end of each section you sew, otherwise your mittens will burst apart when you wear them.

Step 4: Repeat the process with your other glove, but remember to measure against the other hand and set the thumb hole in the same location. Now your mittens are ready to wear!

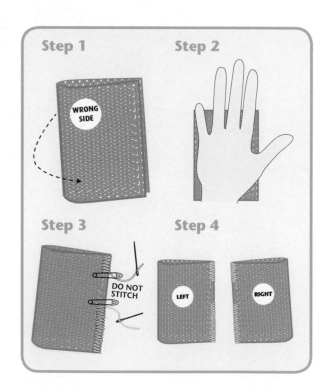

TIP!

If you are adding felt appliqué flowers or shapes, it's easier to sew them on before you make up the gloves.

Place your appliqués so that your gloves are a mirror image of each other, and your design ends up on the back of each hand.

Easy Hats

STITCH
K
Knit Stitch
USED

Baby it's cold outside...time for a nice cosy hat to keep the winter chills at bay! These cute hats are very easy to knit, and are just a simple rectangle shape which we then fold and sew up. We will be using a Knit (K) stitch for every stitch and every row. This is called **Garter stitch**.

Because the hats are very stretchy, the instructions below will make a hat that fits anyone from 6 to 106!

You will need:

1 pair of 4.5mm knitting needles

3 colours of double knitting (DK yarn) —one full ball makes 1 hat so you'll need 3 x 1/3 balls for a 3 colour hat

Piece of card for pom pom

How to knit:

Start off with *colour 1*, **Cast on 50 stitches.**

Knit (K) stitch the first 2 rows.

Change yarn to *colour 2* **(see page 18), knit (K) stitch 2 more rows.**

Change yarn to *colour 3*, knit (K) stitch 2 more rows.

Carry on knitting, changing colour after every 2 rows as before.

Keep knitting until the length of your piece of knitting will go all the way around your head (the stripes should go up and down, not side to side). This could be between 40cm-50cm, depending on the size of head and the thickness of hair.

When your knitting will go all the way around your head, Cast off.

Making up Easy Hats:

Step 1: Lay your rectangle of knitting right side facing up (that's the side that will become the outside of the hat), and with the stripes running up and down. Fold the two outside edges in to the middle to meet each other.

Step 2: Now use mattress stitch (see **page 24**) to sew these two edges together (be careful not to stitch into the back of the hat!) This will make a tube.

Step 3: Now lay the tube flat, with the stitched seam down the middle. Now sew the top two edges together. Turn right side out.

Step 4: The hat will look square when it's flat on the table, but when you put it on, it will look like it has pointy 'ears'! If you like, make a pom pom and pull each ear into the middle and stitch the pom pom in place.

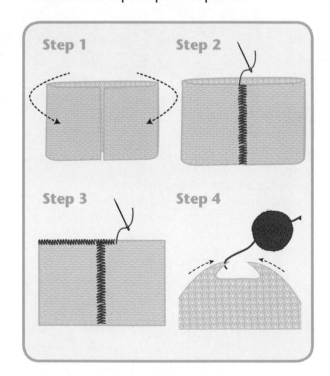

Child's Toy Hat

To make a smaller hat for a teddy or doll, follow the same instructions but Cast on just 25 stitches, and knit until it fits around their head.

Baby Blanket

STITCH
M st
Moss Stitch
USED

The thought of knitting an entire blanket can be daunting to a newcomer — but with a chunky cotton yarn, it will knit up in no time at all.

This blanket uses **British Moss Stitch** — known in the US as **Seed Stitch** — which is a cool combination of alternate knit and purl stitches across each row. Check back to **page 17** for a reminder.

You will need:

I pair of 8mm needles (US size 11)

3 x 100g balls of chunky cotton yarn

How to knit:

Cast On 50 stitches.

Row 1: k1, p1, k1, p1, rep to end.
(Knit a stitch, purl a stitch, knit a stitch, purl a stitch, repeat to end of row

Row 2: p1, k1, p1, k1, rep to end.
(Starting with a purl stitch, you will purl a stitch, knit a stitch, purl a stitch, knit a stitch and repeat to end of row).

Repeat Rows 1 and 2 until your blanket is the size you require.

TIP!
Why not use various colours of yarn to create a striped blanket?
Change colour every 6 or 8 rows, or even use all the primary colours to create a rainbow effect?

Bunny Rabbit Doorstop

STITCH
St st
Stocking Stitch
USED

You will need:

1 pair of 4.5mm knitting needles, plus 1 extra 4.5mm needle

1 ball of chunky yarn

Black felt (eyes and nose), **cute button** (tail)

Needle and thread

Handful of toy filling, pebbles or stones for weight

How to knit:

Knitted in Stocking (St st) stitch — alternate rows of Knit (K) stitch and Purl (P) stitch.

Cast on 20 stitches.

Start off with a row in Knit (K) stitch.

Then bring yarn forward and knit a row in Purl (P) stitch.

Keep going, alternating a Knit (K) row with a Purl (P) row, until you have done a total of 30 rows.

NOW — Knit (K) stitch just 10 of your stitches and stop. In order to "split" the knitting to make ears, we're only going to work on JUST those 10 stitches for now. Place a needle end protector over the other needle to stop those stitches slipping off while you work on the first 10 stitches only. Now grab your spare 4.5mm needle and we can start working on the first 10 stitches.

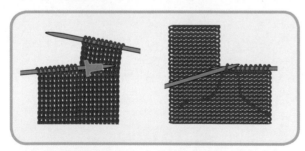

Purl a row, then Knit a row, then keep alternating until you have knit 15 rows altogether. You should end on a Purl row. Now Cast off. You have now made the first bunny ear!

Now let's go back to those other 10 stitches on the other needle.

We need to re-attach the end of the ball of yarn to these stitches so that we can knit them. Slip the end of the yarn through the first stitch and tie a knot.

Now, starting with a Knit (K) row, Stocking stitch (Knit a row, Purl a row) 16 rows in total. Then Cast off.

Hurrah — you have now knitted one side of your bunny. Do the exact same thing again to knit a second side.

Making up Doorstop:

Step 1: It is easiest to sew on the eyes and nose before we sew the two sides together, so cut them out from black felt and stitch on to the right side of one of the bunny pieces (**side 1**).

Step 2: Lay side 1 facing up again, and place the other bunny piece (**side 2**) on top, so that the right sides (what will become the outside of the bunny) are touching. This means you should be looking at the wrong side, the bumpy side, of side 2.

Step 3: Now, using mattress stitch (see **page 22**) sew the two sides together, leaving the bottom section of the bunny open. Remember to secure three stitches on top of each other at the start and end.

Step 4: Now turn your bunny the right way out, and fill 3/4 full with toy filling, pushing right up into his ears. Once full, add some stones or pebbles to the bottom for weight, then stitch the bottom closed securely. To make his ears, tightly tie a piece of yarn around the base and knot securely.

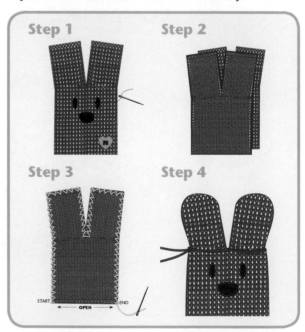

Step 1

Step 2

Step 3

Step 4

START   OPEN   END

TIP!
Why not add a button
or pom pom to make
a cute tail for your bunny?

Beautiful Bunting

STITCH
K
Knit Stitch
USED

This pretty bunting looks great in a bedroom or nursery, or even draped across a fireplace. To make a string of bunting we will need lots of triangles — some small and some large. Before you begin, why not look at **page 21** again to remind yourself how to Decrease stitches. We'll be using Method 1: Knitting 2 Together, also shown as k2tog.

You will need:

1 pair of 4.5mm knitting needles

1 ball of aran yarn in 3 colours (3 balls total)

Yarn or ribbon to join the bunting

Tapestry needle and thread, and pins

How to knit:

We used 10 triangles here, but your bunting could be longer or shorter — it's up to you! Each triangle uses only Knit (K) stitch for each stitch and each row — as you know, this is called **Garter stitch**.

Large triangles

(Make 3 in colour 1 and 3 in colour 2)

Cast on 21 stitches. Knit (K) stitch 4 rows.

 # Knit 2 stitches together (k2tog) at the beginning of the row, then knit as normal until you get to the last 2 stitches, then knit these 2 together (k2tog).

Then knit 2 more rows as normal #.

Repeat these 3 rows from # to # (decreasing at the beginning and end of row 1, knit as normal for rows 2 and 3) until you have just 3 stitches left.

Knit (K) stitch 2 more rows.

Knit first 2 stitches together, knit remaining stitch as normal.

Now Cast off using last 2 stitches and cut the end of the yarn, leaving a short tail. Slip this through the final stitch and pull to tighten.

Sew in end neatly.

Small triangles

(Make 4 in colour 3)

Cast on 11 stitches. Knit (K) stitch 4 rows.

 # Knit 2 stitches together (k2tog) at the beginning of the row, then knit as normal

until you get to the last 2 stitches, then knit these 2 together (k2tog).

Then knit 2 more rows as normal #.

Repeat these 3 rows from # to # (decreasing at the beginning and end of row 1, knit as normal for rows 2 and 3) until you have just 3 stitches left.

Knit (K) stitch 2 more rows.

Knit first 2 stitches together, knit remaining stitch as normal.

Now Cast off using last 2 stitches and cut the end of the yarn, leaving a short tail. Slip this through the final stitch and pull to tighten.

Sew in end neatly.

Making up Bunting:

You now have at least 10 lovely knitted triangles to make into bunting. If you know how to finger knit, make a chain using spare yarn or Cast on 2 stitches and knit a long chain. If you don't fancy either of these methods, you can always use a length of ribbon that matches your triangles.

Step 1: Lay out your ribbon or knitted length, and position your triangles on top so that they are evenly spaced and the colours alternate.

Step 2: Now pin each triangle in place so they stay evenly spaced.

Step 3: Use your needle and thread to sew each triangle on to the ribbon or yarn chain. Remember to begin and end with a knot and a double stitch so you sew each one on securely.

Step 4: You can personalise it by cutting letters from felt and sewing a name onto the bunting!

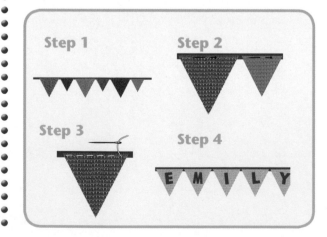

Baby Beanie Hat

STITCH
St st
Stocking Stitch
USED

Unlike some baby hats which are knitted "in the round" using circular needles, this cute baby beanie is knitted with regular needles and sewn together. It also features some 'increasing and decreasing', so it's a wonderful way to progress your knitting skills too.

Using stocking stitch gives the outside of the beanie a nice smooth appearance, and as the lower edge curls up it gives the hat a pretty little rim detail. The cute little leaf is knitted separately and sewn on to the completed hat.

Makes a hat to fit a baby 0-6months.

You will need:

I pair of 3.25mm needles (US size 3)
1 pair of 4mm needles (US size 6)
1 x 100g ball of Cotton Dk yarn (hat)
Small amount of same yarn in green (leaf)
Darning needle

How to knit:

Using your 32.25mm needles, cast on 85 stitches.

Row 1: k85 (knit all 85 stitches)
Row 2: p85 (purl all 85 stitches)
Work the next 4 rows in stocking stitch (knit a row, purl a row)
Change to the 4mm needles.
Starting with a knit row, work in stocking stitch, alternating a knit row with a purl row – until you have a knitted piece of 10cm – ending on a purl row. Now it is time to start reducing stitches to shape the top part of the hat.

To shape the hat:

Row 1: k1, then [k2tog, k4] . Repeat the part in brackets [k2tog, k4] x 14 more times. 71 stitches left.

Rows 2-4: beginning with a purl stitch, work these 3 rows in stocking stitch.
Row 5: k1, then [k2tog, k3]. Repeat the part in brackets [k2tog, k3] x 14 more times.57 stitches left.
Rows 6-8: beginning with a purl stitch, work these 3 rows in stocking stitch.
Row 9: k1, then [k2tog, k2] . Repeat the part in brackets [k2tog, k2] x 14 more times. 43 stitches left.
Rows 10-12: beginning with a purl stitch, work these 3 rows in stocking stitch.
Row 13: k1, then [k2tog, k1]. Repeat the part in brackets [k2tog, k1] x 14 more times. 29 stitches left.
Row 14: purl the entire row.
Row 15: k1, then [k2tog] x 14.15 stitches left.
Row 16: [p2tog] x 7, then purl 1.8 stitches left.

Instead of the usual cast off method, cut the yarn, leaving a long tail – this will be used for sewing up the hat. Pull the tail through the remaining 8 stitches and pull tightly. Now use this yarn to sew the back seam of the hat together using mattress stitch.

To knit the leaves:

Using the same 4mm needles and green yarn, cast on 2 stitches.
Row 1: knit this row
Rows 2-4: increase by 1 stitch at the start of each row (see **page 20**).
Row 5: knit this row
Row 6: k2tog, knit to end of row
Continue to k2tog at the start of each row, until you have 2 stitches left.
Cast off.
Repeat for second leaf and , using the same green yarn, sew securely to top of hat.

k2tog / p2tog

Knit or purl two stitches together, anywhere in a row, to decrease the amount of stitches and shape your hat.

STITCH
St st
Stocking Stitch
USED

This cute little fella will keep your phone or i-pod nice and cosy and safe, AND he uses very little yarn so can be made from leftover yarn in whatever colours you have to hand!

STITCH
K
Knit Stitch
USED

You will need:
1 pair of 4.5mm knitting needles
Aran weight yarn: cream, lilac, green, blue and a tiny bit of black
Tapestry needle for sewing up

How to knit:
Body
With blue yarn cast on 28 stitches.
Knit your first 2 rows in Knit (K) stitch.
Change to lilac yarn, then Knit (K) stitch 2 rows.
Change to green yarn, Knit (K) stitch 2 rows.
Repeat these 6 rows once more: Knit (K) 2 rows in blue, 2 rows lilac, 2 rows green.
Then Knit (K) 2 rows in blue, then 2 rows lilac.
NOW change to cream yarn for the main body of the rabbit.
Knit (K) a row all the way to the end.
Purl (P) the next row.
Now continue to knit (K) a row, then purl (P) a row — so you are doing Stocking stitch, see page 13 — until you have knitted a total of 17 rows in the cream yarn.
Your 17th row should be Knit (K) stitch.
Knit (K) stitch for the next 5 rows.
Cast off, not too tightly!

Ears (*make 2*)
Cast on 16 stitches with cream yarn.
Knit (K) stitch the first 4 rows.
Change to lilac yarn and Knit (K) stitch for 6 rows.
Cast off.
Fold the ear sections in half and sew up the long side so the back of the ear is cream and the front is lilac, when you reach the top of the ears pull your stitching tightly so it forms a more rounded top to the ear, sew your ends in neatly.

Bow Tie
With green yarn, cast on 7 stitches.

Knit (K) stitch for 16 rows.
Cast off.
Fold the section in half length ways to find the centre, take a needle with green yarn and sew running stitch up the middle, pull tightly and wrap wool round the middle 4 or 5 times to form the middle section of the bow tie.

Making up:
Step 1: Lay the main body section of the rabbit so that the Right Side (the outside) is facing up. Use a ruler to find the centre point of the body, then sew the bow tie neatly in place in the centre just above the lilac stripe.

Step 2: Taking black yarn sew two crosses for the eyes, approx 1 inch/3cm down from the top. Then take lilac yarn and sew a "V" shape for the nose in the centre just below the eyes. Finish sewing off neatly on the inside.

Step 3: Now lay the main body section face up so that the RIGHT side — the nice side — is facing you. Fold inwards from each side, so that the left and right edges meet in the middle. This will be the back of the rabbit.

Step 4: Neatly sew the left and right sides together, making sure they meet in the middle of the back of the rabbit. Next sew along the bottom of this section, so that the bottom edges are joined securely too. Turn your Rabbit right sides out now.

Step 5: Place each ear inside the top of the body section approx $^1/_2$ inch/1.5cm down, sew neatly in place, hiding the stitches.

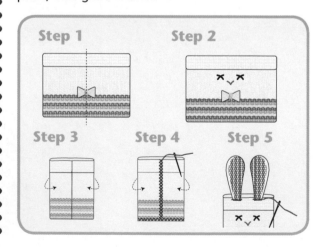

Step 1   Step 2

Step 3   Step 4   Step 5

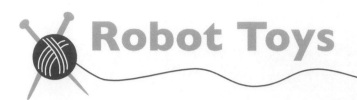

Robot Toys

You will need:

1 pair of 4.5mm knitting needles, plus 1 spare 4.5mm needle

1 ball of chunky yarn in 2 colours (2 balls total)

Black yarn (eyes and mouth), **pink felt** (control panel and nose), **large buttons** (ears), **pretty buttons** (controls)

Tapestry needle and threads

How to knit a Stripy Robot:

If you'd like a stripy robot, follow these instructions. If you'd prefer him to be all one colour, simply skip the parts where you are asked to change yarn colour. These little guys are knitted in Stocking Stitch (Knit a row, then Purl a row).

Robot Body (Make 2)

We will begin knitting at his head:

Cast on 9 stitches in *Colour 1*.

Knit (K) stitch a row, Purl (P) a row, K a row, P a row (4 rows total).

Change yarn to *Colour 2*.

Stocking stitch 4 more rows. Change back to *Colour 1*.

Stocking stitch (K,P) 2 rows.

Shaping the shoulders:

Next row: Before you begin knitting, cast on 3 extra stitches, so that you now have 12 on the needle. Knit (K) stitch these 12 stitches.

Next row: Start by casting on 3 extra stitches, so that you now have 15 on the needle. Purl (P) this row to the end.

Change yarn to *Colour 2*. Stocking stitch 4 rows.

Change yarn to *Colour 1*. Stocking stitch 4 rows.

Change yarn to *Colour 2*. Stocking stitch 4 rows.

Change yarn to *Colour 1*. Stocking stitch 4 rows.

Change yarn to *Colour 2*. Stocking stitch 2 rows.

Shaping the feet:

Now we need to divide our 15 stitches into two sets of 6 stitches, with a gap in the middle. This will allow us to knit individual feet.

Knit 7 stitches, cast off 3 stitches, knit the remaining 5 stitches.

You will now have a total of 12 stitches on your needle, 6, then a gap then 6 more.

Just like we did with the ears for the Bunny Rabbits (page 36), we now need to use our spare knitting needle, so we can work on the sets of 6 stitches separately. Using the spare needle:

Purl the first 6 stitches. Now pop a needle protector on the end of the needle that holds the remaining 6. We'll come back to these later.

Change yarn to *Colour 1*. Stocking Stitch 4 rows. Cast off.

To make the other foot, we will now work on the other 6 stitches.

Re-join the *Colour 2* yarn to the first stitch.

Purl (P) one row, then change yarn to *Colour 1*.

Stocking stitch 4 rows. Cast off.

Well done, you have now knitted one side of your robot. Repeat to knit the second side!

Arms (Make 2):

Starting at the hand, Cast on 10 stitches in *Colour 2*. (continued...)

Beginning with a Knit (K) row, Stocking stitch 4 rows. Change yarn to *Colour 1*.

Starting with a Knit (K) row, Stocking stitch 12 rows.

Cast off, leaving a small tail of yarn for sewing up.

Making up Robot Pals:

Well done, you have now knitted a front and back panel, and two arms. It's time to turn these into a robot!

Step 1: It is easiest to sew on the eyes, nose and control panel before we sew the two sides together, so first use the black yarn to sew some eyes and a mouth onto the front panel of the robot. (Sew on to the right side, which is the smooth side of the knitting). Next cut a nose shape from pink felt and stitch in place. Sew your buttons and shapes on to a square of felt, just like in the picture, then sew this "control" panel on to your robot body!

Step 2: Lay this piece facing up, then place the other robot body piece (side 2) on top, so that the right sides (what will become the outside of the robot) are touching. This means you should be looking at the wrong side, the bumpy side, of side 2.

Step 3: Now, using mattress stitch (see **page 22**) sew the two sides together, leaving the section between the legs of the robot open for stuffing. Turn the right way round and stuff, then sew up the gap.

Step 4: Arms: Fold each arm in half, long-ways, so that the side seams meet. Starting at the hand end, sew the seams together, around the hand and along the long edge. Leave the far end open, turn right side out, then stuff. Sew up the open end of the hand before sewing the arm on to the robot. Now stitch on large buttons for his ears.

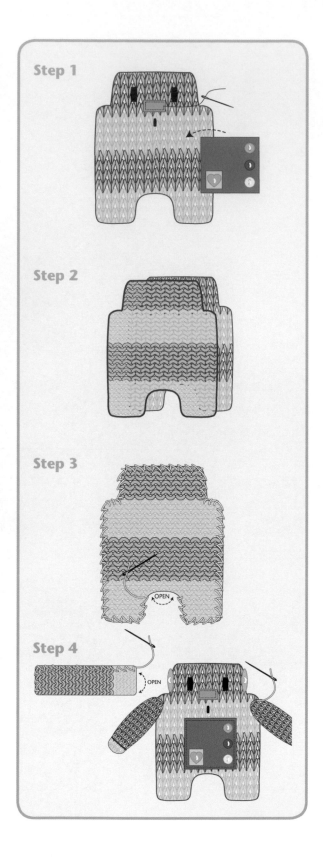

Pet Couture

STITCH
K
Knit Stitch
USED

Fluffy fashions for your favourite friends! When winter strikes, it's not just humans who like to wrap up warm and cosy! These cute accessories take no time at all to knit, and are a great way to try out new stitches or use up leftover yarn.

You will need:

1 pair of 4.5mm knitting needles

Various colours of double knitting yarn (DK yarn) — this will be stretchy when knitted

Piece of card for pom poms

Tapestry needle

How to knit a pet sized scarf:

The width and length of your scarf will depend on what size your pet is.

For cat or small dog — Cast on 10 stitches

For larger dog — Cast on 15 or 20 stitches.

Keep knitting, in whatever stitch you like, until the scarf is just long enough to wrap around your pet.

Cast off.

How to knit a pet sized hat:

To knit a smaller pet-sized hat, we simply follow the instructions for a regular Easy Hat (see **page 32**), but cast on less stitches and knit less rows.

For cat or small dog — Cast on 20 stitches.

For larger dog — Cast on 30 stitches.

Then knit row after row until it fits around their head.

Then sew up and, if you like, add a pom pom to match yours!

SAFETY FIRST

• Always keep a close eye on your pet when wearing as the scarf could become caught or tangled and present a choking hazard.

• Make sure you sew pom poms on VERY securely as they can easily come loose when pets play with them!

More great Craft books from Kyle Craig

I hope you've enjoyed learning to Crochet. Why not learn some new Sewing or Knitting skills with the help of my other books:

Adult Beginner's Books

How To Knit:
A Complete Guide for
Absolute Beginners

How To Crochet:
A Complete Guide for
Absolute Beginners

**How To Use Your
Sewing Machine:**
A Complete Guide for
Absolute Beginners

Kids Books

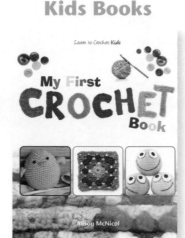

My First Knitting Book

My First Crochet Book

My First Sewing Book

**My First
Hand Sewing Book**

**My First
Sewing Machine Book**

**My First Sewing Machine:
Fashion School**

Search under Alison McNicol for tons more great adult and kids craft books!